SECRETS
OF THE
RAIN FOREST

Carron Brown

Illustrated by Alyssa Nassner

Kane Miller
A DIVISION OF EDC PUBLISHING

A rain forest is bustling with life.

If you look closely at each tree through branches, vines, and ferns and around the huge roots, you will see the animals living there.

Shine a flashlight behind the page or hold it up to the light to reveal what is hidden in and around one tree. Discover a small world of great surprises.

Rain forest trees grow tall with wide trunks and long roots.

Can you see one very tall tree in the forest?

Creak!

The tree has many
branches near the top.

Sunlight shines on the
leaves there.

Many flying creatures rest
high up in the sunny branches.

What's hiding under this leaf?

A beautiful butterfly is resting.

His open wings are larger than
both your hands put together.

Flutter...

Flutter...

Suddenly, the butterfly
flutters into the air.
Other butterflies take
off around the treetop.

Who could have
startled them?

whoosh!

A spider monkey is swinging
through the trees. Her strong
tail clings to branches and vines.

Many plants grow high on the tree.
Their leaves catch raindrops.

Can you see who lives in this
colorful plant?

Splash!

A tree frog and his tadpole
live in a pool of water inside the plant.

Soon, the tadpole will become a frog.

The treetop is a safe place to build a home. It's far away from dangerous animals on the ground.

Who waits in this large nest?

This large chick is a young harpy eagle. Her parents fly to the nest to feed her.

Squawk! Squawk!

Golden lion tamarins
scurry from branch to branch.
They are looking for
tasty insects or fruit to eat.

What are they carrying?

Chatter!
Chatter!

zzz   zzz
            zzz

Baby monkeys ride piggyback.
They're too young to travel alone.

Long, thin vines hang in
a tangle around the tree.
Creatures climb
the woody stalks.

Who looks
like a vine?

A parrot snake is smelling
by sticking out his tongue.

He uses his tongue to
sense food and danger.

Ssssslither!

Most animals race along
the tops of the branches.
Others take their time.

Can you find an
upside-down creature?

Yawn!
A sloth hangs in one place so long that plants grow on her fur.

They turn her coat green.

Colorful flowers bloom in the rain forest.
Animals see their bright shapes.

Who drinks from this red flower?

Whirr!

Hummingbirds
hover by beating
their wings very fast.

Their long tongues
sip sugary liquid
from flowers.

Leafy ferns cover
the ground near the tree.
They make a perfect
place to hide.

Can you see who's
waiting to pounce?

roar!

A jaguar is a big cat
that eats other animals.

He has sharp teeth and claws.

There are more insects than any other
type of animal in the rain forest.

Can you count the leaf-carrying insects?

Snip!

Snip!

A trail of leafcutter ants
are marching to their nest.
The leaves are used to
make food for young ants.

Fallen branches create homes for plants and animals.

Can you see who is inside this plant?

Slurp!

A beetle is trapped inside the slimy walls of a sun pitcher. This plant eats small animals.

A salamander
has spotted danger
lurking in a hollow.

What has he spied
under the rock?

A wandering spider waits
to leap out and catch prey
with one poisonous bite.

Pounce!

There's a
well-trodden path
around the tree.

Can you see who's
walking this way?

Snuffle...
Snuffle...

A tapir is heading to the river for a swim.
Using her long nose, she snatches
up leaves to eat along the way.

The river runs through the rain forest.

Who is making bubbles?

Swish...
Swoosh...

A pink river dolphin uses its large
flippers to swim. It hunts fish,
crabs, and turtles in the water.

As night falls,
the animals who were
busy during the day
fall asleep.

But the rain forest is never quiet.
In the evening, the nighttime
animals wake up. Hundreds of
shining eyes catch the
fading light.

There's more...

Half of all the plants and animals in the world live in rain forests.
There's life everywhere you look.

In the upper canopy The top branches get the most sunlight. Winged creatures such as eagles, parrots, butterflies, and bats, and climbing animals such as monkeys, reach these dizzy heights.

Climbing down The canopy is a tangle of leaves and branches. Rain drips off the leaves, watering flowers and fruits. Many animals live in this food-rich place, including monkeys, sloths, snakes, and tree frogs.

Lower levels It's darker near the bottom of the tree. Sunlight finds a way through the branches for plants such as ferns. Hummingbirds feed on flowers and monkeys climb on the vines.

Roots Large rain forest trees can have huge roots, called buttress roots, that prop up the tall tree. The roots take up water from the soil to help the tree grow. They also take goodness from decaying leaves on the ground.

On the ground Dead leaves and twigs make the forest floor a great place for creepy-crawlies to live, with lots of places to hide and decaying plants to eat. Tapirs feed on the shoots of new plants stretching up to the sunlight.

In the river Many creatures live in the river that winds through the forest, including river dolphins, piranhas, turtles, and caimans. Capybara (the largest rodent), giant otters, and anaconda snakes live both on land and in the river.

Inside plants Spiky plants called bromeliads live on tree branches. Rainwater falls onto their leaves and runs down into a pool in the center of the plant. Some tree frogs carry their tadpoles to a bromeliad pool where they grow into adult frogs.

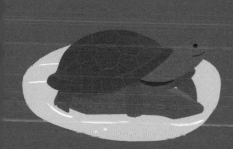

Deadly plants Pitcher plants send out sweet smells that attract insects. Once the creature climbs into the main part of the plant, it cannot get out. The surface is too slippery. The trapped insect is eventually eaten by the plant.

Nighttime At 6:00 p.m., the forest is dark. Some animals are awake only at night. Owls, bats, moths, spiders, and many more creatures start looking for food. Frogs croak, crickets chirp, monkeys howl, and birds screech—nighttime is very noisy!

First American Edition 2014
Kane Miller, A Division of EDC Publishing

Copyright © 2014 The Ivy Press Limited

Published by arrangement with Ivy Press Limited, United Kingdom.
All rights reserved. No part of this book may be reproduced, transmitted
or stored in an information retrieval system in any form or by any means, graphic,
electronic or mechanical, including photocopying, taping and recording,
without prior written permission from the publisher.

For information contact:
Kane Miller, A Division of EDC Publishing
PO Box 470663
Tulsa, OK 74147-0663
www.kanemiller.com
www.edcpub.com
www.usbornebooksandmore.com

Library of Congress Control Number: 2014931069

Printed in China

ISBN: 978-161067-325-9